THE 6 PILLARS OF HEALING: INTRODUCTION

I have had this book written in one form or another for the better part of decade.

My fear of failure and my need to be perfect (in order to be loved and in order to be accepted and validated) held me back from releasing this. I am finally at the stage in my own healing journey, where these wounds have healed, and I am beyond living in that smaller experience. I want a different life, I want to shift, I want to dramatically change my life.

And funnily enough, the steps I took to undergo the change in how I feel about myself and what I can offer, was by using the processes, guides and recordings that are in this book.

Yes, I've used what I am teaching too. These tools and processes really do work. They are a compendium of everything I have learnt through my years of struggling with my own mental health, what I've learnt in therapy, what I have learnt through life, and the insight I have gained through stepping into the spiritual and metaphysical realm.

This challenges limiting beliefs on a psychological level, emotional level, and I have included audio that is purely channelled to help the healing occur on an energetic and vibrational level.

THE IDEA OF THIS BOOK IS TO *RADICALLY* CHANGE YOUR LIFE FOR THE BETTER.

To finally let go of those limiting beliefs that have been getting in the way of you living your fullest life. To shift and transform those beliefs into positive ideals. To clear your mind and energy to make way for powerful creation and manifestation.

You were not meant to go through life in a state of perpetual suffering.

YOU WERE NOT MEANT TO GO THROUGH LIFE IN A STATE OF PERPETUAL SUFFERING.

YOU ARE MEANT
TO KNOW WHAT
LIFE IS LIKE
WITHOUT PAIN.
YOU ARE *MEANT*
TO KNOW
HAPPINESS.

And by the end of this process, my prayer is that you truly and deeply, understand that.

And if at any point you forget that, or another wound emerges that needs your attention, you can use this book gain. You can use this multiple times, and it will still have its value. It's a tool that you can use time and time again throughout your life and your healing journey.

CONTENTS

1
Honesty - Tell the truth

2
Clarity - Get clear about what the issue is

3
Root - Define the root cause for this belief and problem

4
Release - The process of truly letting go

5
Affirm - Transforming negative into the positive

6
Create - Manifest from a new point of power

1.
HONESTY
-TELL
THE
TRUTH

In order to truly heal and overcome your pain, you have to first be honest about what is actually wrong. You can't get over a problem by denying its existence. The fact you've bought this book means you've got a pretty good idea that somethings up!

You might not be able to admit it to other people, ashamed there's something the matter, or even find it hard to admit to yourself. However, the way this starts is by you telling the truth. About how you really think and feel.

You may have never done this before, you might feel quite comfortable not looking directly at your issues or problems, but let's face it – not looking at them and denying their existence is not working for you. Ignorance in this case is NOT bliss. Ignoring your problems in this case will eventually cause your life to come to a crashing halt, (if it hasn't done already) and then you will HAVE to face them all head on.

This will feel strange at first, and you might be completely stumped to begin with. "I don't know what my problem is, I'm just fucked up". That actually means there's plenty to dive into, you just haven't let yourself have the time to sit and stare directly into your shadows.

So, why not do it before the giant car crash? Yes, I agree, that is a much better option.

Right now, we don't have to be too specific, you can be general, but specific enough that you get a sense of where your issues sit e.g. I'm not confident anymore, I have problem speaking up, I don't like my body, I'm scared of failure etc.

Spend as little or as much time on this as you wish, but you've got to be honest about it. Use this space or your own pen and paper to really get it all out.

If I'm really honest with myself, my biggest issues right now are :

Well done for admitting the truth to yourself, and for being brutally honest with yourself. I know that it isn't always easy, it's much easier to go about pretending that everything's Ok, settling for just getting by, but one of the reasons you bought this course, is because you're sick of being stuck in survival mode. You want peace, you want happiness, and you deserve it too.

Once you understand your blocks, and break down those beliefs into manageable segments that you can sort through, you start to become very aware about what your core issues might be.

2.
CLARITY - GET CLEAR ABOUT WHAT THE ISSUE IS

Now that you've expressed the issues that you're experiencing, it's time to narrow it down, to just one problem. The big kahuna. The thing that really gets in the fucking way of you progressing and enjoying your life.

Deep down you already know what this actually is. If you reflect back on the notes you made in the previous section, you will be able to see a repeating theme with each issue.

As complex as each of our pasts may be, made up of so many different experiences, we are not so individual when it comes to the issues. If you read through all the things that you put down as your problems, you will be able to categorise them under one umbrella. Your core issue that is behind each of these will be one of the following-

"I am not enough"

"I am not loveable"

"I am afraid of failure"

"I am not important"

"I am not safe"

"I am powerless"

_____

When reading through that list, one of those will have hit differently to all the rest. They are very simplified versions of complex feelings most of us have towards ourselves, but we have all felt each of those at varying degrees at various points in our lives. Which one triggered the biggest response within you as you read it? Does it cause the same response within you if you say it out loud? If you could make the sentence longer, does it feel more true to you? For example,

"I put everyone else's needs before mine, like I am not important"

"I feel anxiety everywhere I go, I feel like I am not safe"

"I need to be perfect all the time, I am so afraid of failure"

"I hate my body, I don't have a relationship, I feel like I am not loveable as I am"

"I don't want to put myself out there, I don't feel good enough; I am not enough"

In my own experience, my biggest blocks were feeling like I wasn't enough i.e. I am not enough, and feeling that I had to be perfect to be loved, and therefore I wasn't loveable just as I was, so again, I am not enough.

So when you read through those sentences, and apply them to you personally and your situation, which do you feel the strongest?

The one I feel most deeply is :

3. ROOT - DEFINE THE ROOT CAUSE FOR THIS BELIEF AND PROBLEM

Ask yourself, when was the first time I ever felt this? When did I first believe this to be true? Give it a moment, and sink into the feeling.

_____

Normally the first instance that comes to mind is the one that started it all. Don't rush yourself, take some deep breaths and really remember the first instance you took on board these beliefs.

I understand some of our pasts are quite traumatic and problematic, where memories can be blurred or completely erased. If you are someone that empathises with this, just go with the memory that stands out the most. A time when you most deeply felt your statement to be true.

Once you have your memory figured out, try to remember the details surrounding this. What did you feel at the time? What did it make you think? What could you see? What did you perceive to be true? Use the space provided or your own pen and paper to take some time now to journal about this:

When you look back on this, I want you to view this from two different stand points. Here is an example from my own experience to help you:

When my dad left, it made me feel awful. I felt so unlovable, I just couldn't be enough to make him stay. Even if I was perfect, he was still going to leave. I just wasn't enough. I couldn't do anything to stop it. I felt deserted and that I wasn't good enough for the male figure in my life.

This filtered through and affected my self-esteem and my confidence. I hated myself, I never felt enough, and I never thought I could be enough for any man, even if I was perfect it still wouldn't be enough. (Note how one event, has reverberated out into so many different areas?)

Reflecting back on the situation from a different perspective, how I felt and what was true were very different. What I learnt from the situation was that I wasn't good enough. I embodied the belief 'I am not enough' and 'I am not lovable'. Obviously, these are false reflections of the truth of the matter. What actually happened, is my parents' marriage had broken down before I was even born, and their divorce was inevitable, and there was nothing on my part that I could ever do about that. Him leaving the marital home had absolutely nothing whatsoever to do with me. In fact, he adored me.

But my younger self didn't know all of that, that was outside the limits of my comprehension at the time.

Yet now, I can see the full picture, and understand that my thought of "I am not enough" was based upon false beliefs. It just wasn't true. So if my thoughts were based on things that weren't true, that must mean that the thought itself can't be true.

"I am not enough" just isn't true.

IT
CAN'T
BE
TRUE.

How freeing is that? To finally see the full picture for what it actually is? To clearly see that those thoughts just aren't true. To surmise, this also means that whatever thought you had, can't be true either. It's just what you believed with all the information you had **at that time.**

With that in mind, use this space or your own pen and paper, to objectively write about the facts surrounding your memory that created your core issue:

Can you see now, that what you believed to be true, and what actually was, are two very different scenarios? This is powerful to recognise the stark difference between the two. It creates a shift and separation between yourself and those ideas. Enough distance to be able to see that that view point is no longer serving you, that perspective will no longer be a filter you view your whole life through.

THAT
PERSPECTIVE
WILL NO LONGER
BE A FILTER YOU
VIEW   YOUR
WHOLE   LIFE
THROUGH.

_____

If you are a trauma survivor, and this doesn't feel like it relates to you:
Your core beliefs that have been instilled in you would be either, or both of the following –

"I am not safe"
"I am powerless"

What happened to you is unforgiveable. What happened to you is tragic. What happened to you was not your fault. You did not attract it. You were abused. You were a victim. Someone in a point of power and authority decided to treat you the way that they did and it was wrong. It was abhorrent. The damage that was caused has been a pain that you have carried as a burden ever since.

Even though what happened shook you to your very core, there is a power inside of you that is relentless. Your spirit is powerful. Your soul has survived. You have survived. You are powerful. Probably more powerful than most. You have a strength within you that is unmatched. You are incredible. You are a miracle. You are here now. You are here now. You are safe now.

And to help you untether your soul from those painful experiences, the next section includes a divinely channelled piece of audio to incur the healing on a metaphysical level.

4.
RELEASE - THE PROCESS OF TRULY LETTING GO

There will already have been some shifts made just by recognising the thought pattern and where that belief originated from. Some distance between yourself and the feeling, but those thoughts still remain. The vibration still left in your energy.

Now is where we do the work to release these from all of the energy systems. When I talk about energy systems, I am referring to your physical body, your conscious mind, your aura and chakra centres, and the imprints on your spirit and soul. In order for an issue to stop impacting your life, it must be removed from all of these energy systems. Mind, body and spirit. If the energy work isn't done to back up the practical inner work, the problem almost always finds a way of hanging around.

For this, I have channelled healing to help you release this from your system, and as you listen to and breathe along with me, you will feel the emotions rise up, you will feel the sensation of pain leaving your body, you will experience a seismic shift that will utterly transform your outlook and wellbeing.

Scan the QR code to listen

You are not defined by what happened to you. You are no longer controlled by what happened to you. You are no longer held back by what happened to you. That vibration is no longer in your energy. Those feelings are no longer inside of you. Every cell in your body welcomes peace. Every fibre of your being is open to love and possibility.

5. AFFIRM - TRANSFORM THE NEGATIVE INTO THE POSITIVE

Now we've let go and released, there's a lot of space now. There's potentiality in the gaps where pain once resided. It's in this new found freedom that you can now transform your once negative beliefs about yourself and life, into positive encouraging affirmations.

Creating positive affirmations is a great way to help you shift your life, but I strongly believe that they don't hold as much power until you've moved out the old. Otherwise the statements just feel false,

"I deeply and completely love myself"
whilst thinking - "Yeah right, whatever"

"Money flows easily to me" whilst thinking -
"I'm fucking *broke*, but whatever"

If you try and incorporate positive affirmations into your daily practice without first shifting the underlying issues, they just make you feel even worse about yourself and your current situation. Luckily, through this work, you have already released the baggage and are ready to adapt into a new way of thinking and believing.

If you don't feel you're fully ready yet, go back and do the releasing stage once more, or twice more until you actually feel that you have in fact, let go.

Re-listen to the healing and releasing audio as much as you need to before you are ready for the next stage of the process.

Let's use my own example as a starting point, as I know many people can relate to not feeling that they are enough.

"I am not enough" can relate to so many different aspects of life, so you may wish to alter this as it pertains to money, relationships, career etc. The relevance it held for me, made sense that my positive affirmation to counter this negative belief would be:

"I am enough, just as I am. I do not need to prove my worthiness. I am worthy, I am loveable, I am enough just as I am"

_____

You may choose to use that if it feels right for you, or you can shift it around until it clicks. What matters is that it makes sense and feels right for you. And right now, you might not be ready to state something fully positive like "I love myself" and that is absolutely fine! You can rework your affirmations as much as you need to, and right now, if what you are satisfied with is -

"I am healing, I am learning to love myself, I'm doing my best and that's OK"

_____

Then that is absolutely OK! Affirmations only benefit you if they feel true to say in your current state. The over stretching will put you in a place of not feeling good, and that's not what we're after. Healing means going at your own pace, not rushing it, taking your time and fully caring for yourself at each stage. Use this space or your own pen and paper, to transform your negative thought patterns into positive affirmations that feel right for you right now.

NEGATIVE THOUGHT
PATTERN → POSITIVE
AFFIRMATION

NEGATIVE THOUGHT PATTERN → POSITIVE AFFIRMATION

You can come back to this and use this format as often or as little as you like. You might create a new positive affirmation that straight away feels amazing, and you go on to use that in your daily spiritual practice. Or, you come back weekly to alter it slightly to feel aligned with where you feel you are currently. It's entirely up to you, I can't stress this point enough, it must feel right for you.

Use these affirmations, say them during your meditations, write them on your mirror, set them as reminders on your phone. Whatever way works for you, integrate them into your day. It's not just creating affirmations for the sake of them, to look positive or whatever. These are to replace your old thinking patterns. These are to guide your thoughts and choices. These are meant to positively affect and change your life.

Here is a channelled journey of transforming affirmations designed to uplift and transform your state:

Scan the QR code to listen

6.
CREATE-MANIFEST FROM A NEW POINT OF POWER

The magic of healing is that once you've released and removed damaging blocks from your energy, you are now able to create and manifest from a new powerful perspective. The things you've let go of, the thought patterns you used to hold, shaped and moulded your life.

How long did thinking that you weren't enough hold you back?

How many times did that stop you from making different choices?

How different would your life look if you embodied your new powerful affirmations and beliefs for the next 2 years?

For the next ten years?

Where would you be?

What would that look like?

What would that feel like?

WHAT   WOULD
THAT   LOOK
LIKE?

WHAT   WOULD
THAT *FEEL* LIKE?

_____

Hold onto that feeling - that sensation running through your body as you envision your most perfect life, is the absolute key to manifesting. Let it completely flood your system, and define what your most beautiful life would be. Use the space provided or really let it flow using your own pen and as many pages as you like:

Whilst your nervous system is flooded with all these magical feelings, listen to this channelled session to unlock your manifesting potential:

Scan the QR code to listen

Hold onto how fucking fantastic you feel right now. This is how your life could feel every day. Just by putting your body and mind into alignment with these incredible feelings, you are creating a powerful point of attraction whereby you can magnetise and manifest so fast, you'll laugh when things arrive into your life. They will emerge and arise at such perfect points in such imaginative ways, you'll blow your own mind. The universe can, and will, surprise and delight you in ways you can't even fathom.

You are deserving, and have always been worthy, of a beautiful happy life. Just because your life used to be difficult, doesn't mean it has to be anymore. Life is about to get so, so good for you. You are no longer controlled by what happened to you. You are no longer held back by what happened to you. Give yourself permission to be free.

ALLOW AND ACCEPT THAT.

AND SO IT IS.

LET IT BE.

_____

Printed in Poland
by Amazon Fulfillment
Poland Sp. z o.o., Wrocław
02 March 2023

b5f0e805-e037-4b18-8488-db77549dc20cR01